حَميميّات

Intimate Verses

Maximes Intimes

Vertraulichkeiten

Henri Zoghaib

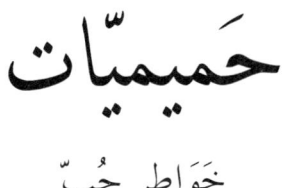

خَواطِر حُبّ

Intimate Verses
English translation:
Adnan Haydar and **Michael
Beard**

Maximes Intimes
Version française:
Rouba Saba Habib

Vertraulichkeiten
Übertragung ins Deutsche:
Ursula Assaf-Nowak

Published by
Dynamic Graphic, Publishers
Jounieh, Main Square, Adem Bldg.
P.O. Box: 261, Jounieh, Lebanon
dynamic@cyberia.net.lb
Copyright © 2008 Dynamic Graphic, Publishers

First Syracuse University Press Edition 2008
08 09 10 11 12 13 6 5 4 3 2 1

Published in the United States by Syracuse University Press
Syracuse, New York 13244-5160

For a listing of books published and distributed by
Syracuse University Press, visit its Web site at
www.SyracuseUniversityPress.syr.edu.

ISBN -13: 978 0 8156 0925 4
ISBN -10: 0 8156 0925 6

Library of Congress Cataloging-in-Publication Data

Zoghaib, Henri, 1948–
[Poems. Selections. Polyglot]
Hamimiyat : khawatir hubb / Hinari Zughayb = Intimate verses =
Maximes intimes = Vertraulichkeiten / Henri Zoghaib ; English
translation Adnan Haydar ; version française Rouba Saba Habib ;
Übertragung ins Deutsche Ursula Assaf-Nowak.
p. cm.
ISBN 978-0-8156-0925-4 (pbk. : alk. paper)
I. Haydar, Adnan. II. Beard, Michael, 1944– III. Habib, Rouba
Saba. IV. Assaf, Ursula. V. Title. VI. Title: Intimate verses. VII.
Title: Maximes intimes. VIII. Title: Vertraulichkeiten.
PJ7876.O35A1995 2008
808.8'1'1— dc22
                                  2008061113

Manufactured in Lebanon by Dynamic Graphic Publishers

U.T.

إليكِ

العنوانُ أنتِ

الطريق

والوصول

U.T.

For you …

the destination is you
so is the road
and the arrival

U.T.

A Toi et pour Toi

Ma parole
dont
tu es l'Intitulée
la Voie
et l'Arrivée

U.T.

Für Dich …
die Anschrift bist
Du,

PREFACE

It is only appropriate that a collection of very short poems should be accompanied by a very short introduction. But how do you make an introduction short? As translators we are fascinated by the kind of work the poet must have exerted to make his text as brief and intense as the one you have in this little book. It seems to us it is work that might require a long essay to explain.

Take the first poem:

رُؤْيِالُ.ِ... فــأرى

Ru'yâ-ki ... fa-ara

Ton présage ... et je te vois.

Eine Vision von dir ... Ich sehe.

A vision of you. Therefore I see.

How can we demonstrate the substance condensed there, whether we call it content, elegance, emotion, meaning, or style? We could start by thinking of the poem as an ideogram: a simple sentence containing a noun, a possessive ending, an ellipsis, the conjunction "fa" (a single letter in Arabic: "then," "and so," "thus," "hence," "so that" - any number of set-ups implying addition, a copula, or cause and effect), plus a first-person verb. Do we have room for some grammar? "Ru'yâ" is a verbal noun, from ra'a, "he saw," and the possessive suffix, -ki, is the feminine of "your." So far it is a rather abstract claim – "your vision," "a vision of you." (A slight variation, "ru'yatu-ki," another verbal noun, from the same stem, would have given us "seeing you.") Things become more interesting when we consider that "ara," which concludes the poem, is a different version of the same verb.

The English version took one possible path through the possible implications. "Vision" in English can mean either an illusion or a reality. The French translator, with "présage" and an ellipsis, suggests something oracular, even a revelation, as in "ru'yâ Yûhannâ," the Book of Revelations in the Bible, since a présage suggests a glimpse of the future. The French opts for "fa" as a simple copula, "et," whereas the German, with no conjunction at all, puts the reader in a position to supply it. "Vision," a Latinate loan word in German, may hint at something slightly exotic in the person that the speaker of the poem is looking at, and the absence of a conjunction to echo that slight Arabic "fa" may make the ellipsis carry a particular weight. The English translators took the contrary direction, opting for a more specific conjunction, "therefore" (with that glance at Descartes), a conjunction so specific that we felt it made the ellipsis unnecessary. None of us were able to find in the resources of our languages a verbal noun echoing the "I see" as cunningly as "ara" echoes "ru'yâ."

A short introduction. It may be enough to allow the reader to imagine the long one. Multiply by one hundred to deal with all Henri Zoghaib's poems. Multiply by four hundred if we wanted to account for all the permutations. Commentary has its own pace, and sometimes the translators are as anxious as the readers to turn the page and arrive at the poems themselves.

Adnan Haydar and Michael Beard

The illustrations
are by artist
Wajih Nahle

رسوم الكِتاب المِئة

مُختاراتٌ من مراحلَ فنيةٍ مُختلفة

قدَّمَها الى الشاعر

صديقُه

الفنان وجيه نَحلة

❖ 1 ❖

رُؤْيِالُكِ... فـنَأَرَى

A vision of you.   Therefore I see.

Ton présage ... et je te vois.

Eine Vision von dir ... Ich sehe.

❖ 2 ❖

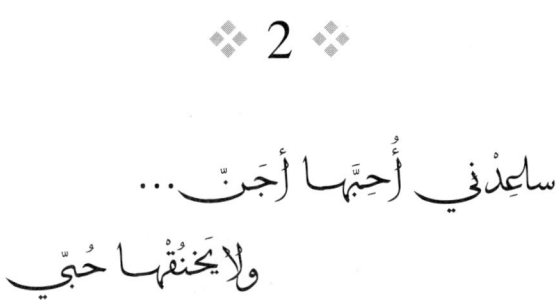

Help me madden myself in her love
short of smothering her.

Secours-moi dans son amour
J'en deviendrais fou.
Que mon amour ne l'étouffe point!

Hilf mir, sie in meiner
leidenschaftlichen Liebe
nicht zu ersticken!

❖ 3 ❖

التَعَبُّدُ لَكِ، لا العبادة.
هيَ، حـالةٌ مَوروثة.
هوَ، فعـلٌ إرادىّ.

Devotion to you, rather than worship:
an inherited state.
Devotion is a willful act.

Te vénérer, non t'adorer
Ceci est un héritage.
Celà est un acte volontaire.

Verehrung für dich, keine Anbetung;
dies ist ererbt,
jenes ein Willensakt.

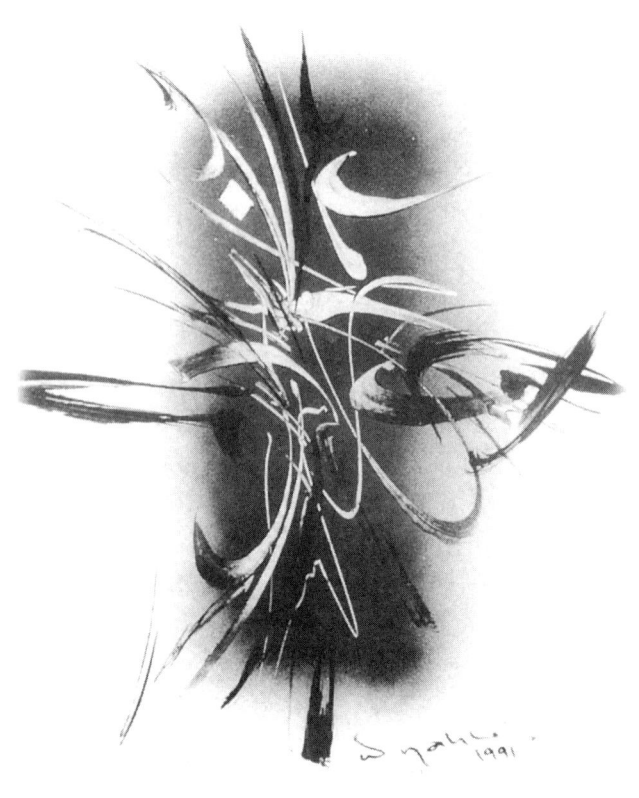

❖ 4 ❖

قَدَمَالُكِ... مَمْلَكَتي.

Your feet, my kingdom.

Tes pas ... Mon royaume.

Deine Schritte ... Mein Königreich.

❖ 5 ❖

بِجَمالِكِ أُقْسِمِ... يَطْهُرُ القَسَمِ!

It is on your beauty that I swear.
Your beauty makes swearing pure.

Par ta beauté je jure ...
Et le sermon se purifie!

Auf deine Schönheit schwöre ich ...
Der Schwur wird rein.

❖ 6 ❖

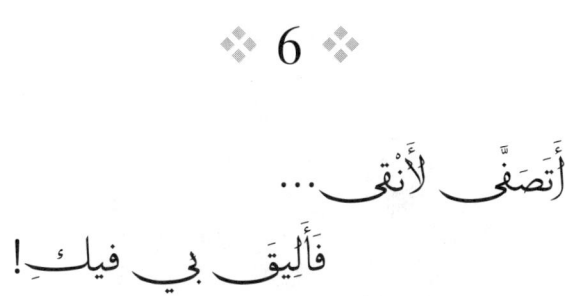

أَتَصَفَّى لأَنْقى ...
فَأَلِيقَ بِي فِيكِ!

I sift through every flaw in me
in order to distill pure worthiness for you.

Je me purifie, je deviens plus limpide …
Je me complais en toi.

Ich läutere mich …
um deiner würdig zu sein.

❖ 7 ❖

أَبُوسُ جَبِينَكِ ...
أَعلُو إِلى تُراث بلادي.

Just to kiss your forehead elevates me.
I become a citizen of your universe
my homeland, my heritage.

Quand j'embrasse ton front
J'accède au patrimoine de mon pays.

Deine Stirn küssend ...
erreiche ich das Erbe meines Landes.

❖ 8 ❖

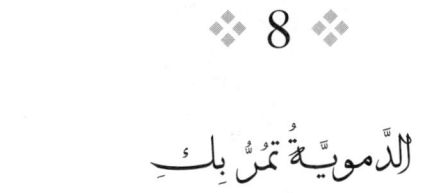

دَوِرَتي الدَّمويَّةُ تمُرُّ بِكَ
قبـل أَنْ تَعُودَ إلِيّ.

My blood as it circles passes through you
and only then gets back to me.

Bien avant qu'elle me revienne,
Ma circulation sanguine passe par toi.

Mein Blut kehrt erst zu mir zurück,
nachdem es durch deine Venen kreiste.

❖ 9 ❖

هويّةُ عالمي أنتِ... وفئةُ دَمِه.

The identity card of my world is you.
My blood type is UT positive.

Toi: L'identité de mon univers …
La catégorie de mon sang aussi.

Du bist der Personalausweis meiner
Welt ebenso wie meine Blutgruppe.

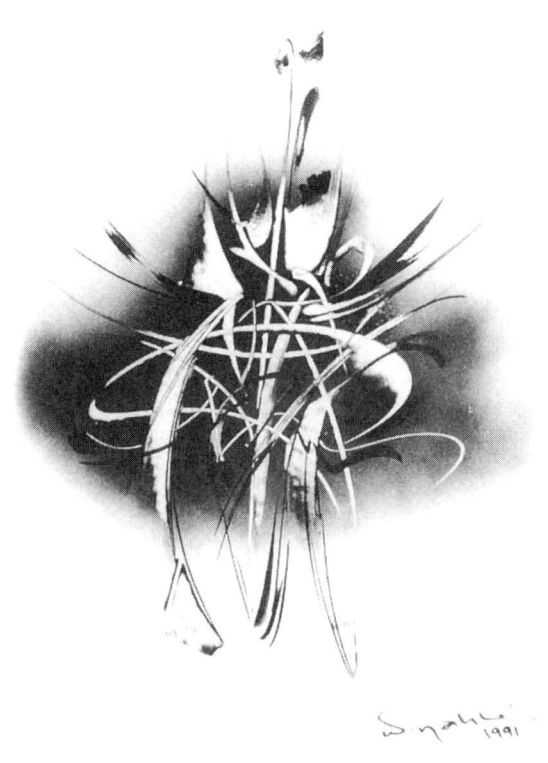

مــا أنتِ في الـ"هُـنـا"؟؟؟

مُشَرَّدٌ أنا في كُلّ هُناك.

Are you not in the here and now?
I am a vagabond in every there.

Tu n'es pas dans l'ici???
Je suis l'errant dans tout ailleurs.

Du bist nicht im Hier?
Ich vagabundiere in jedem Dort.

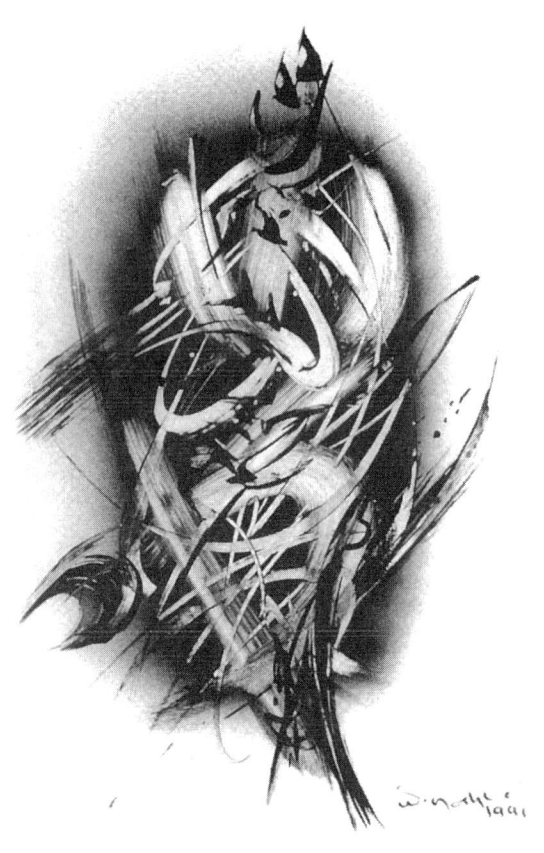

في كَفِّكِ عُشبةٌ مِن حقلي؟؟؟
ها ربيعي على أنامِلكِ تَقَمَّص.

Even the weed you pluck from my garden
reincarnates the entire season of spring
on your fingers.

Dans la paume de ta main
Une herbe de mon champ???
Voici mon printemps,
sur tes doigts, incarné!

Ein Grashalm meines Feldes
in deiner Hand
verkörpert den Frühling
auf deinen Fingern.

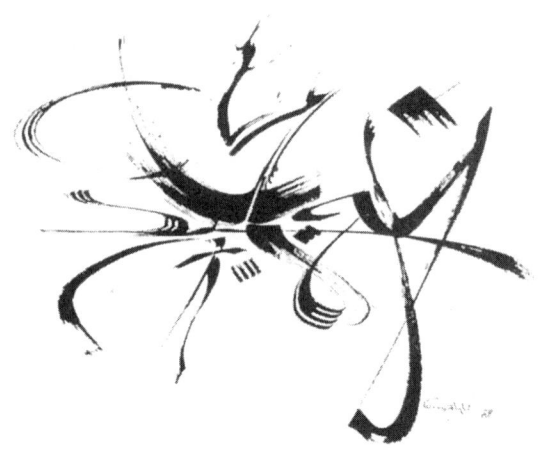

❖ 12 ❖

للتفكيرِ بكِ... رائحةُ المستقبلِ!

The mere thought of you – a fragrance from the future.

Te penser ... Parfum du futur!

Ein Gedanke an dich ... Duft der Zukunft.

❖ 13 ❖

للصباحِ سببٌ آخر: صوتُكِ.

ولليلِ لونٌ آخر: صَداكِ على صدري!

Your voice:
one more reason for morning to arrive.
The night has one more color:
your bright echo on my chest.

Ta voix:
une autre cause du matin
Ton écho sur ma poitrine:
L'autre effet de la nuit!

Deine Stimme: ein anderer Grund
für den Morgen.
Dein Echo auf meiner Brust:
eine andere Farbe der Nacht.

❖ 14 ❖

جمالُكِ خُبزِيَ اليومي.

Your beauty, my daily bread.

Ta beauté ... mon pain quotidien.

Deine Schönheit ... Mein tägliches Brot.

❖ 15 ❖

سعادتي مَعَك... قُوَّة.

My happiness with you ... my strength.

Force ... mon bonheur avec toi.

Meine Stärke ... Mein Glück mit dir.

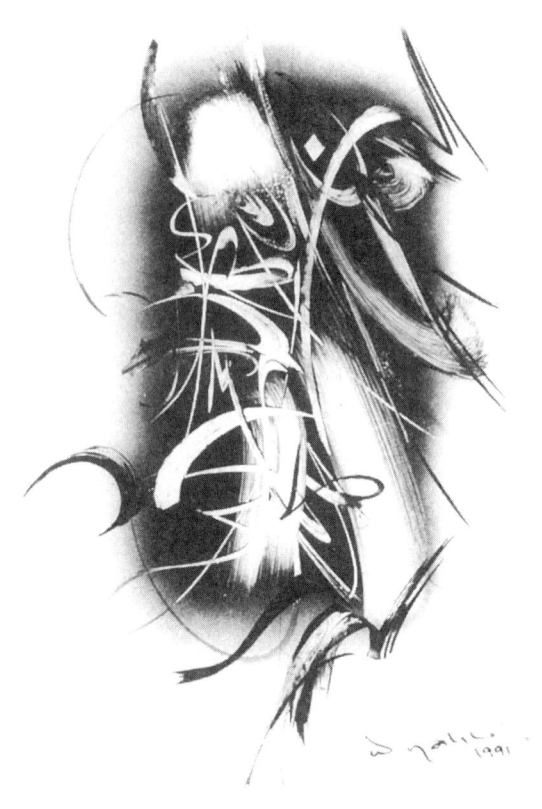

❖ 16 ❖

رَحْمُكِ... أَمِ الزّنبق؟

Your womb, or the tulip?

Ton utérus ... ou bien le lys?

Dein Schoß ... oder die Lilie?

 **17**

All the strength I have ...
the glow from my devotion to you.

Toute force en moi ...
Aura de mon attachement à toi.

Alle Kraft in mir ...
die Glut meiner Verbundenheit mit dir.

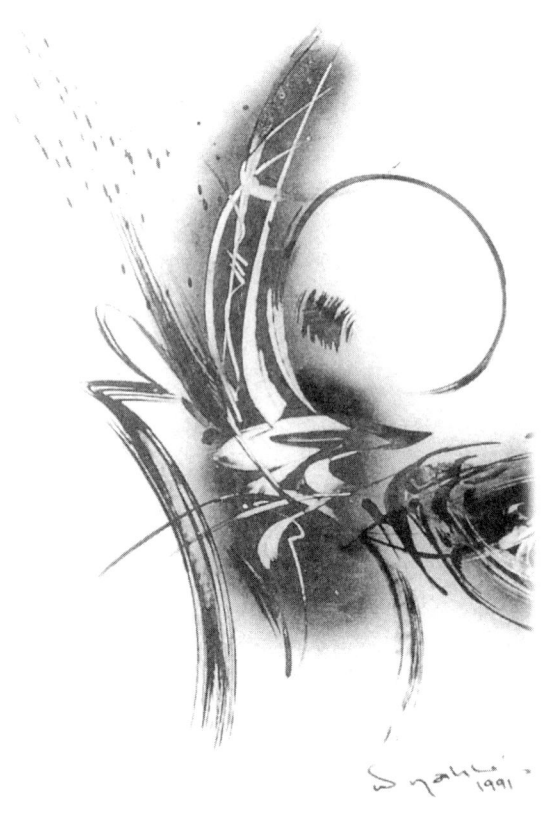

❖ 18 ❖

حين لا تنظرين إليَّ،
أَتَمَتَّع بقراءةِ عينيكِ أوضَح.

When you look away from me
I enjoy reading your eyes more clearly.

Quand tu ne me regardes pas,
Je me délecte d'une lecture plus claire
de tes yeux.

Wenn du mich nicht ansiehst,
ergötze ich mich an einer genaueren
Lektüre deiner Augen.

❖ 19 ❖

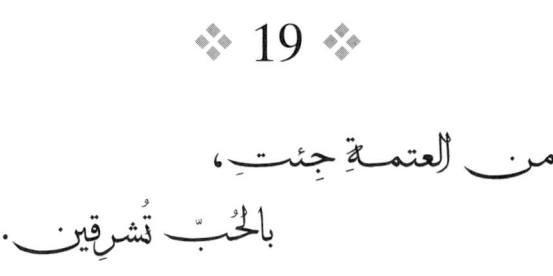

من العتمةِ جئتِ،
بالحُبّ تُشرقين.

You come from darkness,
your love my every morning's light.

De l'obscur tu viens,
Par l'amour tu rayonnes.

Du kamst aus dem Dunkel
und leuchtest durch die Liebe.

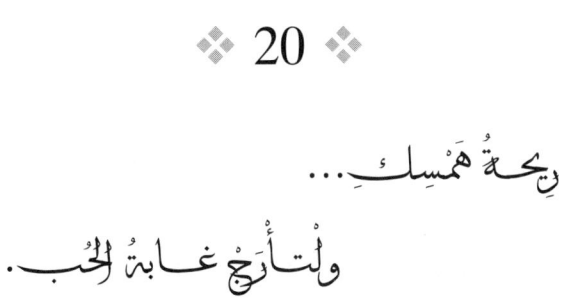

... رِيحَةُ هَمْسِكِ
ولْتَأَرَّجْ غَـابةُ الْحُبِّ.

The fragrance of your whisper
and love's forest rustles with perfume.

Parfum de ton murmure ...
Que la forêt d'amour s'arôme!

Der Hauch deines Geflüsters,
und der Wald der Liebe duftet.

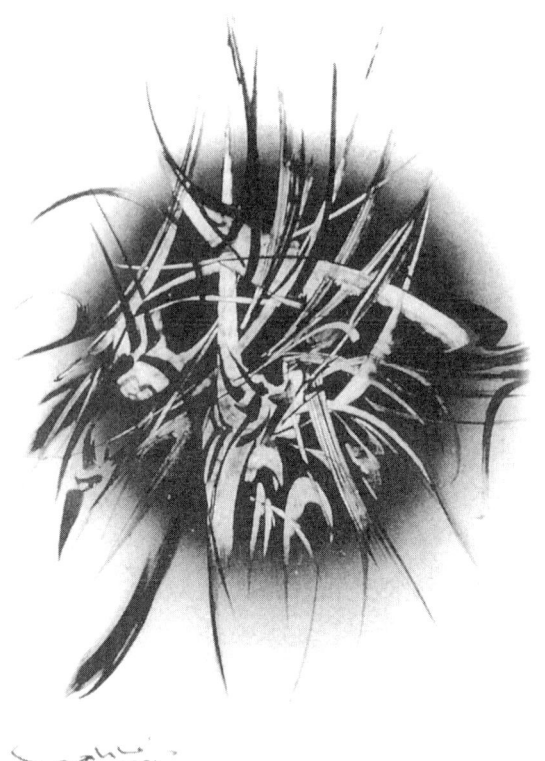

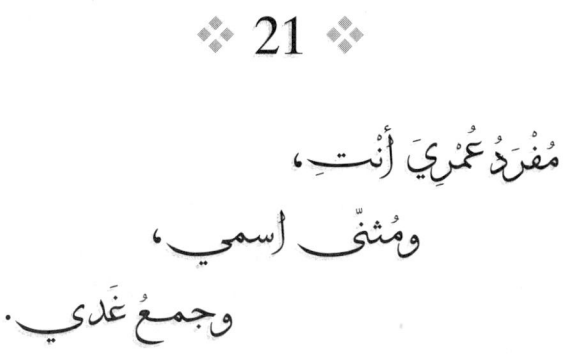

21

My life in the singular: you.
My name in the dual form: also you.
My tomorrow in plural? Still you.

Mon âge, tu-es, singulier
Mon double, prénommé
Le pluriel de mon lendemain es-tu?

Mein Leben im Singular bist du,
mein Name im Dual
und der Plural meines Morgen: du.

❖ 22 ❖

لا أَنَّكِ تُحِبِّينَنِي ، بـل... كيفـ.

It isn't that you love me.
It's how.

Non, Toi tu m'aimes!
Plutôt, Comment?

Nicht, daß du mich liebst, ist es;
vielmehr wie du mich liebst.

❖ 23 ❖

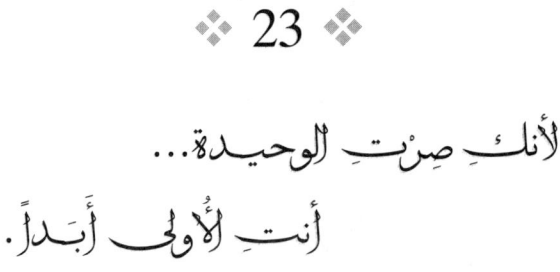

لأنكِ صِرْتِ الوحيدة...
أنتِ الأُولى أبَداً.

Now that you're the only one
you'll always be the first.

L'unique, tu es devenue,
Te voilà première pour toujours.

Da du die einzige wurdest,
wirst du stets die erste sein.

❖ 24 ❖

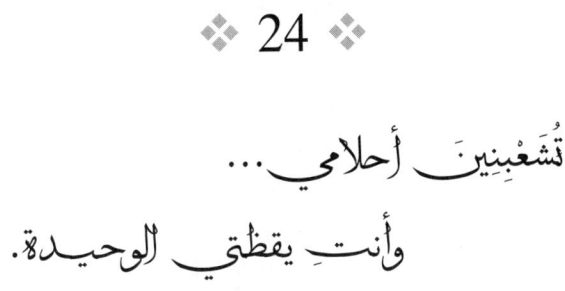

تُشَعْبِنِينَ أحلامي ...

وأنتِ يقظتي الوحيدة.

Although
you populate the nations of my dreams
I emigrate to you, my constant
awakening.

Tu peuples mes rêves ...
Car tu es mon seul réveil.

Du lebst in meinen Träumen
und bist mein einziges Erwachen.

❖ 25 ❖

أُنوثَتُكِ السُّلطَةِ والقِيـادة،
ورُجولَتي في الطـاعة والحَنان .

The woman in you,
authority and command,
the man in me,
pliancy and tenderness.

Du pouvoir et de l'orientation;
ta féminité,
Ma virilité:
dans l'obéissance et la tendresse.

Deine Weiblichkeit:
Autorität und Befehl;
meine Männlichkeit:
Gehorsam und Zärtlichkeit.

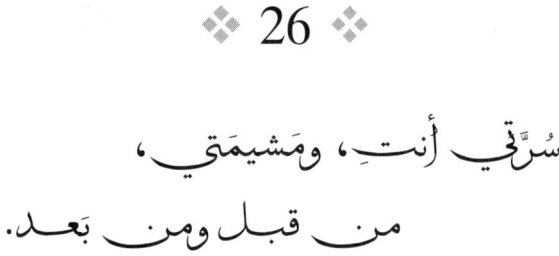

سُرَّتي أنتِ، ومَشيمَتي،
من قبل ومن بَعـد.

You are my navel cord,
my placenta,
connecting before with after.

Mon cordon ombilical;
Mon salut placentaire,
D'avant et d'après
Tu es.

Du bist der Nabel meines Lebens,
du verbindest das Vorher mit
dem Nachher.

❖ 27 ❖

في قلبكِ / الرحم،
أَتَقَمَّص منْكِ إِلَيْكِ.

Your heart – the womb
from which I am reborn,
from you to you.

Utérus, ton cœur,
Je m'incarne en toi
envers toi.

In Herz und Schoß wiedergeboren
von dir zu dir.

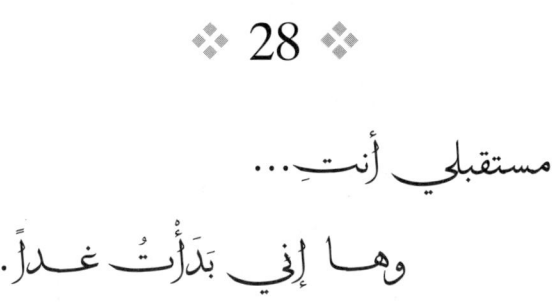

❖ 28 ❖

مستقبلي أنتِ ...
وهـا إني بَدَأْتُ غَـدَاً.

My future is you.
And lo – here I begin tomorrow.

Mon futur tu es ...
Me voilà demain, commencé!

Meine Zukunft bist du.
Mein Morgen hat begonnen.

❖ 29 ❖

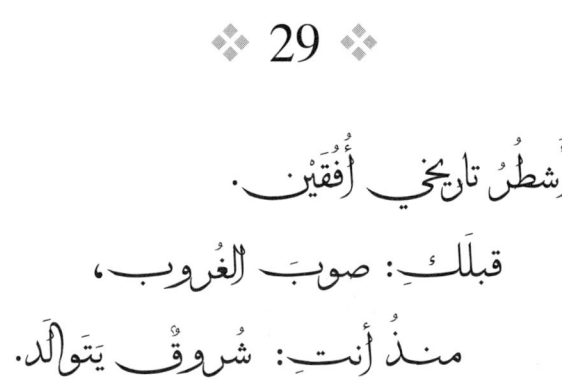

أَشطُرُ تاريخي أُفُقَين .

قبلَكِ: صوبَ الغُروبِ ،

منذُ أنتِ: شُروقٌ يَتوالَد .

I slice my history into two horizons.
Before you was towards the setting sun.
Since you, sun fathers sun before my eyes.

En deux horizons, je tranche mon histoire.
Avant toi: vers le crépuscule
Depuis toi: lever du jour qui régénère.

Meine Geschichte teile ich in zwei Horizonte.
Vor dir: Sonnenuntergang
Nach dir: dauernder Sonnenaufgang.

❖ 30 ❖

دائرةٌ...
أنتِ بي نقطتَها والمحورِ .

You form a complete circle
both the dot at my center
and the circumference.

Orbite en moi
Tu en es le point et l'axe.

Ein Kreis ... Du bist
der Mittelpunkt und die Achse.

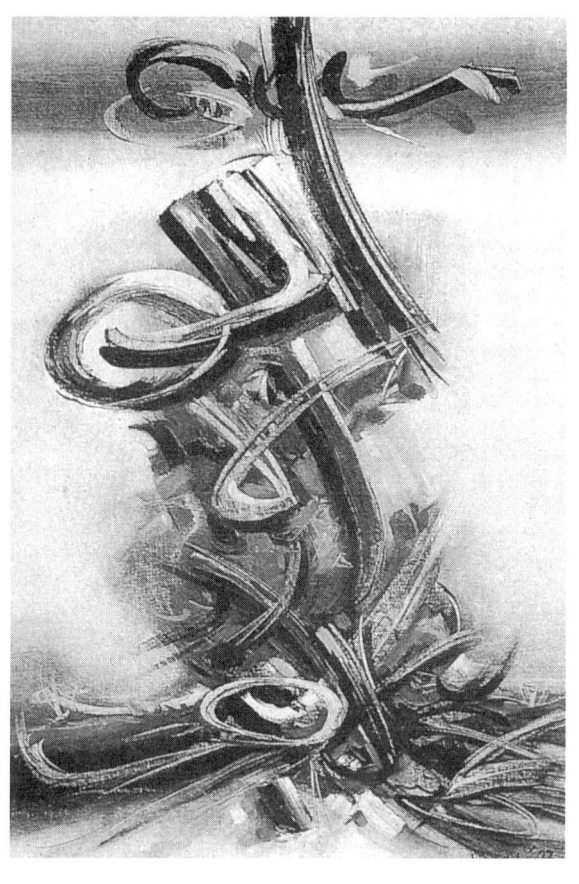

❖ 31 ❖

إِنقيادي إِليكِ... حُرِّيَّتي.

My freedom is traced
by my obedience to you.

Me soumettre à toi ... ma liberté

Mich dir zu unterwerfen ...
ist meine Freiheit.

❖ 32 ❖

دمي أنتِ... أعيريني شرايينى.

You are my blood ...
loan me my own artery
and we'll merge as one.

Mon sang serais-tu
Prête-moi mes veines.

Mein Blut bist du ...
leihe mir meine Venen!

❖ 33 ❖

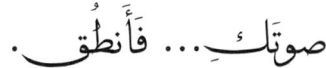

Your voice ...
so I can speak.

Ta voix ...
Et je profère ma parole.

Deine Stimme ...
und ich kann sprechen.

❖ 34 ❖

جَمَالُكِ... وَلْيَـأْرَجِ اليَاسَمِينـ.

Your beauty
tells the jasmine when to breathe.

Par ta beauté,
Le jasmin embaume.

Deine Schönheit ...
und der Jasmin duftet.

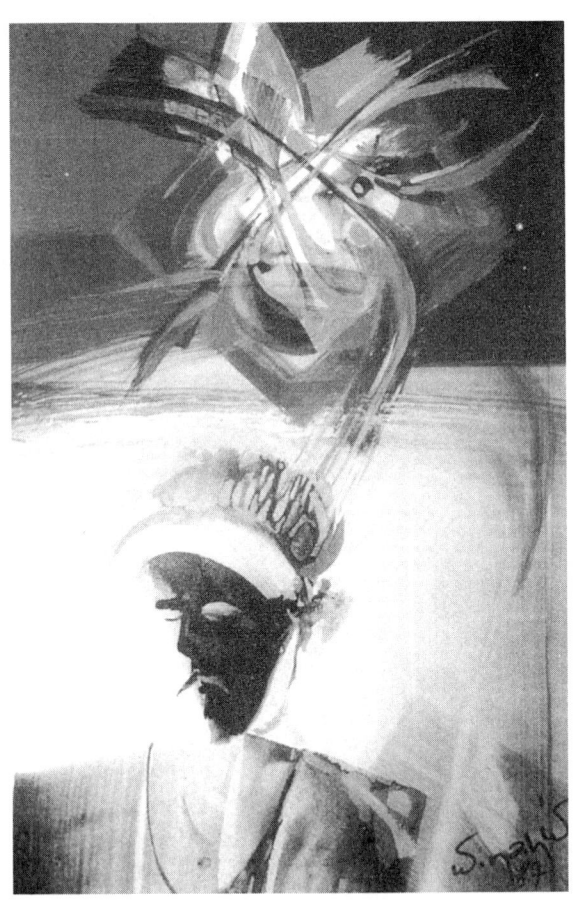

❖ 35 ❖

وَجْهُكِ... أَعْمَاراً لأَقْرَأ.

Your face would take me
many lives to read.

Ton visage ...
Des âges pour ma lecture.

Dein Gesicht ...
mehrere Leben, um es zu lesen.

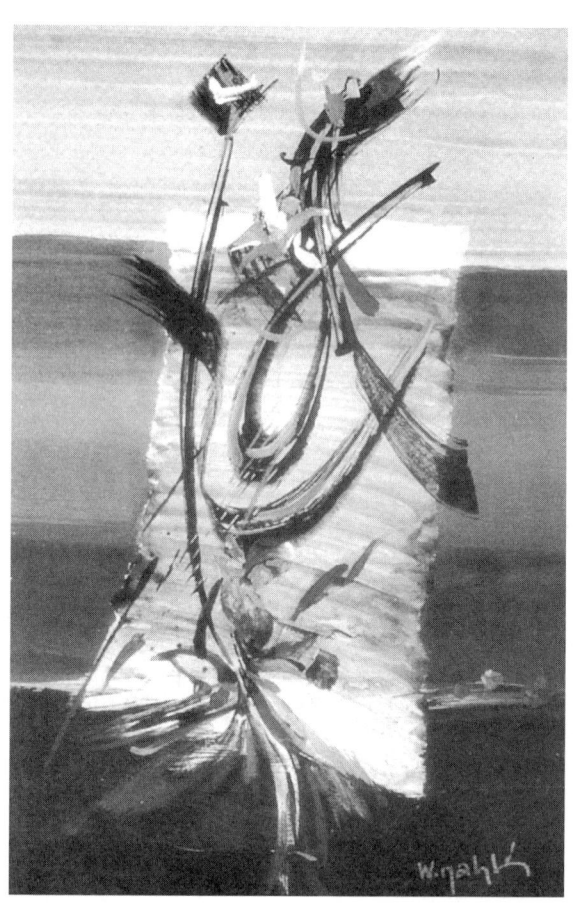

❖ 36 ❖

نقاؤُكِ مرآتي... فـلا أَخْجَل.

I look into your purity like a mirror.
It helps me overcome my shame of me.

Mon miroir: ta limpidité
Je n'ai plus honte.

Deine Reinheit ist mein Spiegel ...
ich schäme mich nicht.

❖ 37 ❖

أَتَأَمَّلُني أُحِبُّكِ... أُغبِطُني.

I look closely at myself in love with you.
I envy myself.

Je me contemple, comme je t'aime
Je reste béat.

Ich betrachte mich in meiner Liebe
zu dir ... ich beneide mich.

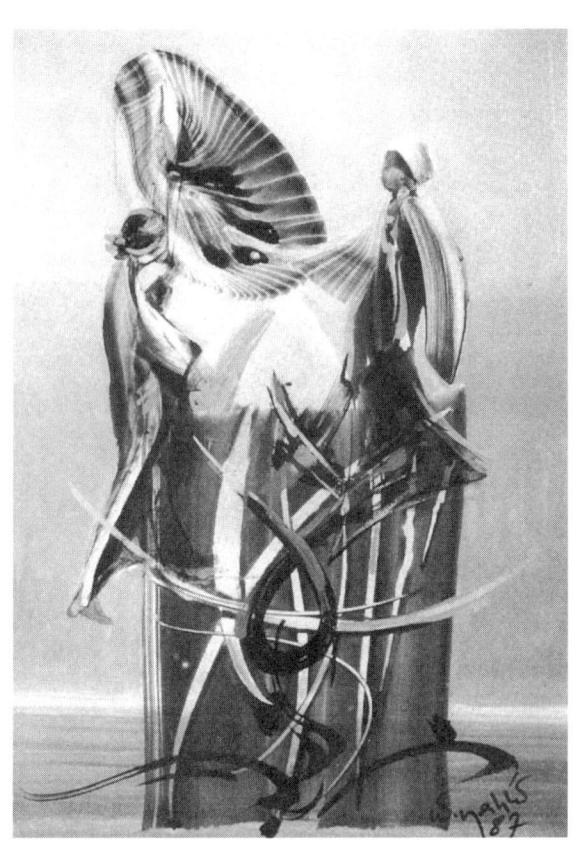

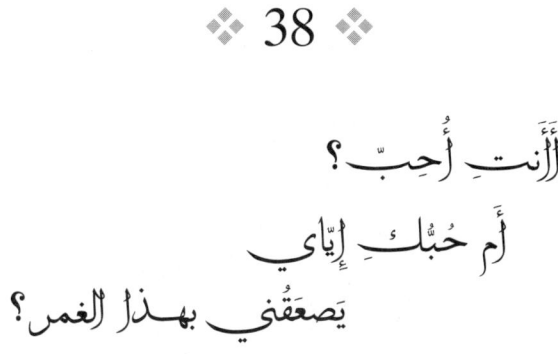

أَأَنتِ أُحِبّ؟
أَم حُبُّكِ إِيّاي
يَصعَقُني بهـذا الغمس؟

Is it you I love or am I simply stunned
by this deluge from your love?

Es-ce l'amour que j'ai pour toi
Ou bien ton amour pour moi
Qui me foudroie autant?

Ist es meine Liebe zu dir oder deine Liebe,
die mich überwältigt ?

❖ 39 ❖

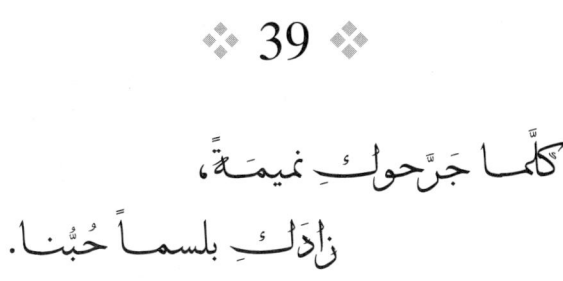

كُلَّمـا جَرَّحوكِ نميمَةً،
زادَكِ بلسمـاً حُبُّنـا.

The more their idle speech wounds you
the better our love will cure those wounds.

Quand tu es blessée par la rumeur,
Notre amour agira sur toi comme un baume.

Immer wenn ihre Verleumdungen dich
verletzen, wird der Balsam unserer Liebe
die Wunden heilen.

❖ 40 ❖

قبلَكِ ...
كانت المرأةُ لي جسداً وروحاً.
منذُ أنتِ... صارتِ امرأةً.

*Before I knew you, "woman" meant to me
body and soul.
Since you, it's just woman.*

*Avant toi ...
La femme était corps et âme.
Depuis toi ... Elle est Femme.*

*Bevor ich dich kannte,
war die Frau für mich Körper und Geist.
Seitdem ich dich kenne ist sie Frau.*

❖ 41 ❖

طَاعَتُكِ أُمُّ انصِياعِي.

Obeying you gives birth to submission.

Ton obéissance à moi
Matricité de mon consentement.

Dein Gehorsam ist der Grund
meiner Unterwerfung.

❖ 42 ❖

شَجَنٌ في صوتِكِ؟ أيُّ غُروبِ!

Is that sorrow in your voice?
Sadness at sunset.

Affliction dans ta voix?
Quel crépuscule!

Besorgtheit in deiner Stimme?
Welch ein Sonnenuntergang!

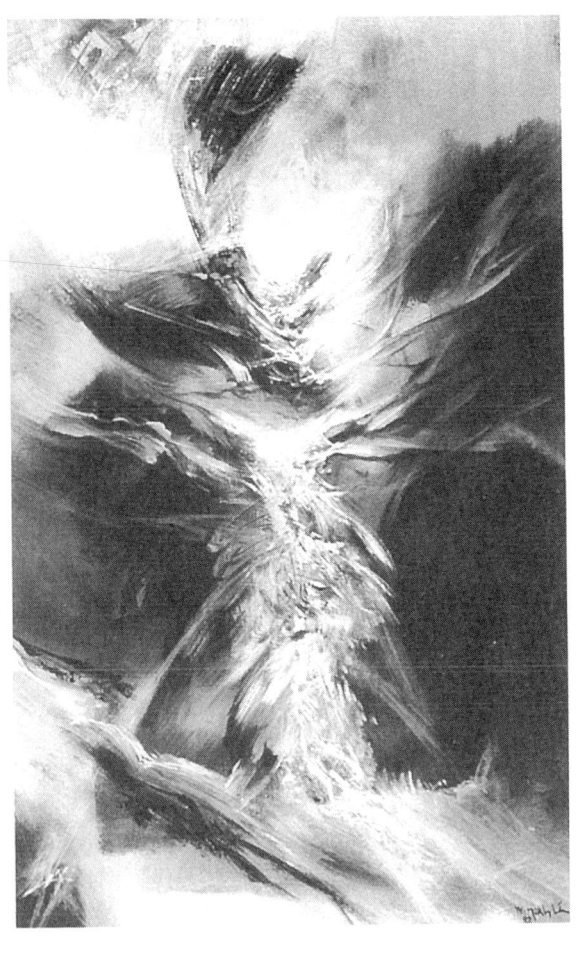

❖ 43 ❖

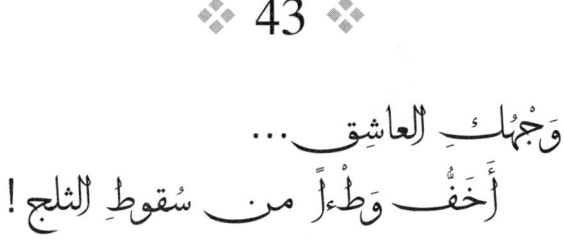

وَجْهُكِ العاشِقِ ...
أَخَفُّ وَطْءاً من سُقوطِ الثلج !

One affectionate glance from you
lighter than the footsteps of falling snow.

Ton visage passionné d'amour
Plus feutré que la chute des neiges.

Dein liebevolles Gesicht ...
leichter als Schneefall.

❖ 44 ❖

لِجَمَالِكِ هَمْسٌ بِلَونِ الياسَمين !

Your beauty whispers
in the color of jasmine.

Le chuchotement de ta beauté
a du jasmin; le ton.

Deine Schönheit flüstert
in der Farbe des Jasmin.

❖ 45 ❖

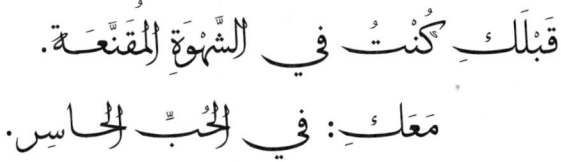

قَبْلَكِ كُنْتُ فِي الشَّهْوَةِ المُقَنَّعَـة.
مَعَكِ: فِي الحُبِّ الحَاسِر.

Before you came I wore the mask of lust.
Now you're here and my love is unveiled.

Avant toi, j'étais dans le désir masqué.
Avec toi: dans l'amour dévoilé.

Vor dir trug ich die Maske der Lust;
mit dir ist meine Liebe unverschleiert.

❖ 46 ❖

جَمالُكِ زِنْبقٌ.
والزَّنبقُ يُصان.
لا تُهْملِيـه.

Your beauty is a white tulip.
Don't bruise it.

Liliale ta beauté.
Et le lys se sauvegarde.
Ne le néglige pas.

Deine Schönheit eine Lilie.
Vernachlässige sie nicht!

أَشُمَّهُ... أَشُمَّهُ...

يَضُوعُ الصّبـاحِ.

كيفَ وَجْهُكِ فَجْرٌ !

I fill up with the perfume of your face.
And so
your face is savored by the coming dawn.

Je l'hume ... Je l'hume ...
Le matin embaume.
Comme ton visage est une aube!

Ich atme ihn tief ein,
den nahenden Morgen.
Dein Gesicht ... die Morgenröte.

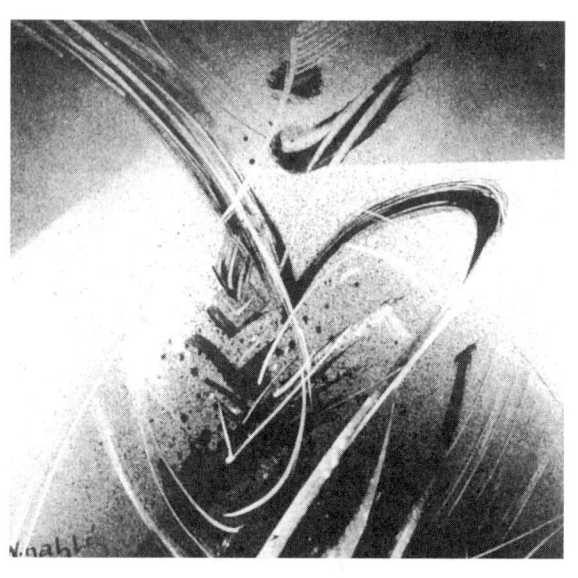

❖ 48 ❖

بَيْنِي وَيَيْنِي ذَاتُ: أَنتِ !

There you are,
a self between myself and me.

Entre moi et le Moi: toi tu loges.

Zwischen meinem einen
und anderen Ich: Du.

 49

Your candor embarrassed me.
I've become pure.

Ta sincérité m'intimidait …
Je me suis purifié.

Deine Aufrichtigkeit beschämte mich.
Ich bin geläutert.

❖ 50 ❖

شَقِيٌّ بِـدونِ رِضاكَ. أَلْبِسِينِيـهِ.

Without your blessing I am bare.
Clothe me in it.

Dépourvu, misérable,
Sans ta bénédiction.
Habille-moi d'elle.

Ohne deine Bestätigung bin ich bloß.

❖ 51 ❖

أَنتِ؟ أَمِ القصيدةُ؟

أَعِيرِينِي وَجْهَكِ لأَقرأ.

Is it you or the poem?
Lend me your face that I might read.

Toi? ou le poème?
Prête-moi ton visage pour lire.

Du oder das Gedicht?
Leihe mir dein Gesicht, damit ich lese!

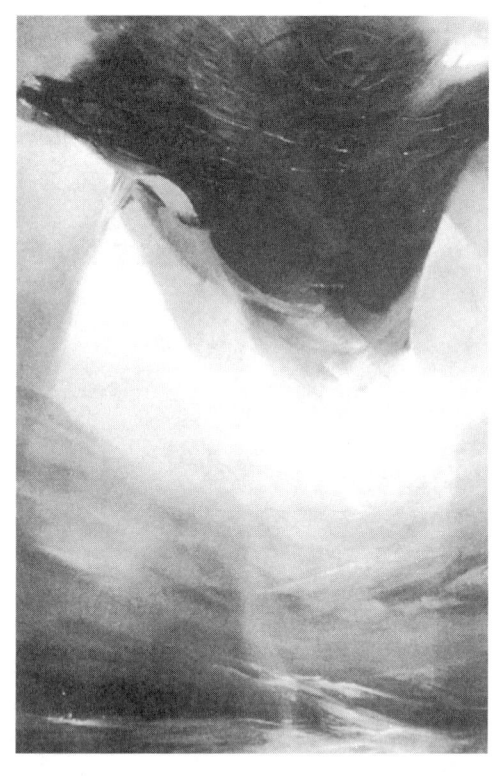

❖ 52 ❖

... U.T.

عيـدُ مولِدي أنتِ

... كُلَّ صبـاح !

U.T. My day of birth.
Every morning.

U.T.
A chaque matin
Tu es mon anniversaire.

U.T. Mein Geburtstag
an jedem Morgen.

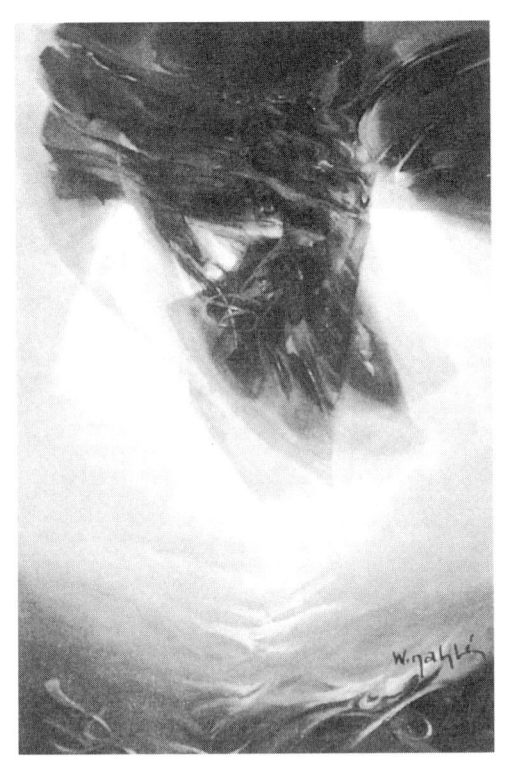

❖ 53 ❖

أَوَّلُ الجُـذورِ ... قَدَمالكِ. أَكْمِلِينِي.

Your feet ... where love takes root.
Let me flower.

Avènement des racines ... tes pas.
Prolonge-moi.

Deine Schritte ... Erste Wurzeln.
Lass sie spriessen!

❖ 54 ❖

كيفَ لا أُخْجَلُ من ضآلةِ نجومي إِليكِ...

وأنتِ الجَلَد؟

You are the whole sky.
My faint stars embarrass me.

Comment n'ai-je pas honte de mes
astres ternis vers toi,
Alors que tu es le cosmos?

Wie schäme ich mich nicht meiner
wenigen Sterne für dich ...
Und du bist der ganze Kosmos.

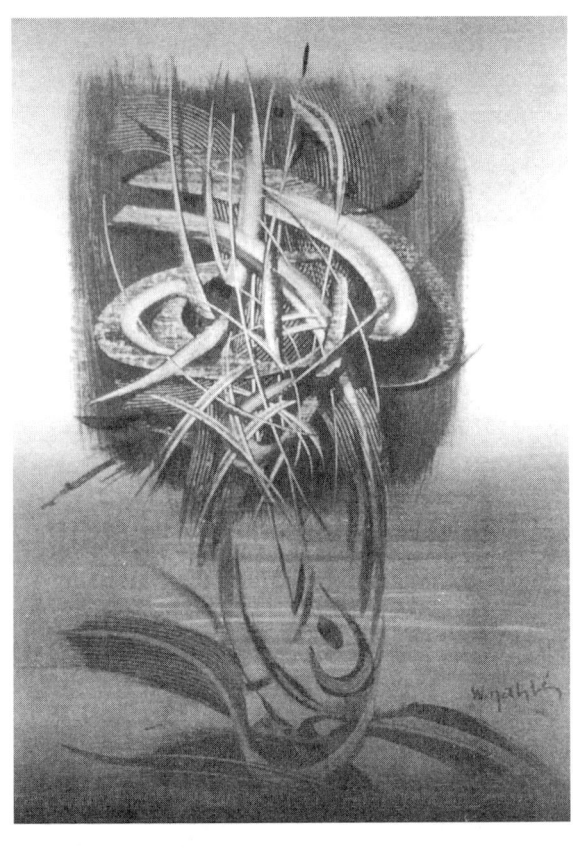

❖ 55 ❖

جمرةُ الشوق تهـدُ بين الشفتين،
يَنِزُّ العسـلُ المـالح.

Embers of desire simmer
between your lips.
A comb of honey and of salt too.

La braise du désir bourdonne entre
les lèvres.
Ruisselle un miel salé.

Die Glut der Sehnsucht zwischen
deinen Lippen.
Ein Geschmack von Honig und Salz.

❖ 56 ❖

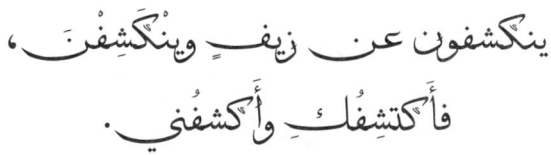

ينكشفون عن زيفٍ وينْكَشِفْنَ،
فأَكتشِفُكِ وأَكشفُني.

Once laid bare men show their falseness.
Women too.
I show mine when I discover you.

Par le mensonge,
Ils se dévoilent, elles aussi.
Je te découvre, je me démasque.

Männer und Frauen entpuppten
sich als falsch.
Doch als ich dich erkundete,
entdeckte ich mich.

❖ 57 ❖

أُولَدُ فيكِ كلَّ صبـاحٍ...
وأُحيـا بينكِ وبينكِ.

In you every morning I'm reborn.
Thus I span my life between you and you.

En toi, chaque matin, je renais
Entre toi et toi-même, j'ai à vivre.

In dir werde ich jeden Morgen neu geboren.
Ich lebe zwischen dir und dir.

هــذا الضوءُ... هــذا الضوءُ...
وجهُكِ أم وهُجُكِ؟

That light out there, that light ...
is it some passing radiance
or is it your face?

Cette lumière ... Cette lumière ...
Ton visage,
ou bien ton incandescence?

Dieses Licht ... dieses Licht ...
Ist es dein Gesicht oder deine Glut?

❖ 59 ❖

أَتَمَلّاكِ ولا أرتوي... ويغمرني النبـع.

My eyes fill up with you
only to thirst again ...
you, my overflowing spring.

Je m'adonne à ta contemplation,
Je reste inassouvi.
Et la source m'enveloppe.

Ich betrachte dich.
Mein Durst bleibt ungestillt,
trotz der Quelle, die mich überflutet.

❖ 60 ❖

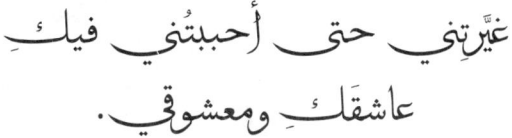

غَيَّرْتِني حتى أُحببتُني فيكِ
عاشقَكِ ومعشوقي.

You transformed me,
and now I can love
myself in you ...
Your lover and my own.

Tu me transmutes
Au point que je m'aime en toi;
Amant et Objet de mon propre désir.

Du verwandeltest mich. Nun liebe
ich mich in dir.
Liebhaber und Geliebter zugleich.

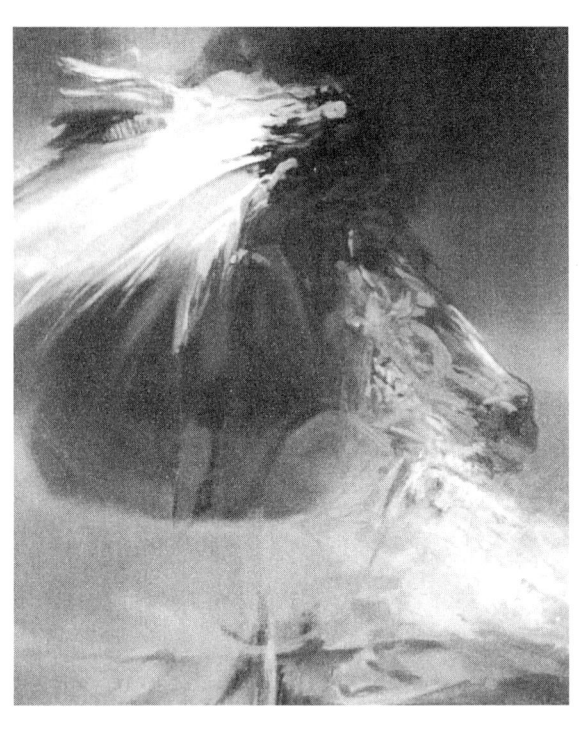

❖ 61 ❖

كلّ صباحٍ نَبْضُكِ أُكْثُ...

فمـا أَنْضَرَ عمري !

The morning sees your heartbeats grow.
Within me my deep green years
will grow with their increase!

Chaque matin,
ta pulsation en moi s'accélère.
Oh! Qu'il est juvénile mon âge!

Jeden Morgen,
ist dein Pulsschlag schneller.
Wie jugendlich ist mein Alter!

❖ 62 ❖

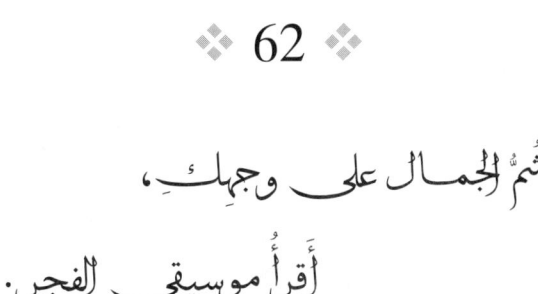

أَشُمُّ الجَمــالَ على وجهِك،
أَقرأُ موسيقى الفجر.

I breathe in the beauty of your face.
I am able to read the music of dawn.

Je sens la beauté de ton visage,
Je déchiffre une musique aurorale.

Ich atme die Schönheit deines
Gesichts ein
und lese die Musik der Morgenröte.

❖ 63 ❖

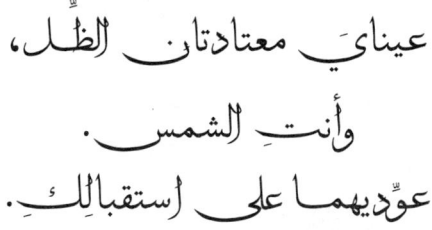

My eyes are used to shade.
And you are the sun.
Make welcoming you their habit.

Mes yeux ont l'habitude de l'ombre.
Tu es le soleil.
Apprends leur à t'accueillir.

Meine Augen sind den Schatten gewohnt.
Du aber bist die Sonne. Lehre mich,
dich willkommen zu heißen.

❖ 64 ❖

كتاباتي قبلَكِ مقدّمات.

منـذ أنتِ: تقدمات.

*Before I knew you, everything I wrote
was just a preface.
With you, the story begins.*

*Mes écritures avant toi:
Des avant-dires.
Depuis toi: des offrandes.*

*Alles, was ich vor dir schrieb,
war Einleitung.
Was ich seitdem schreibe, ist Widmung.*

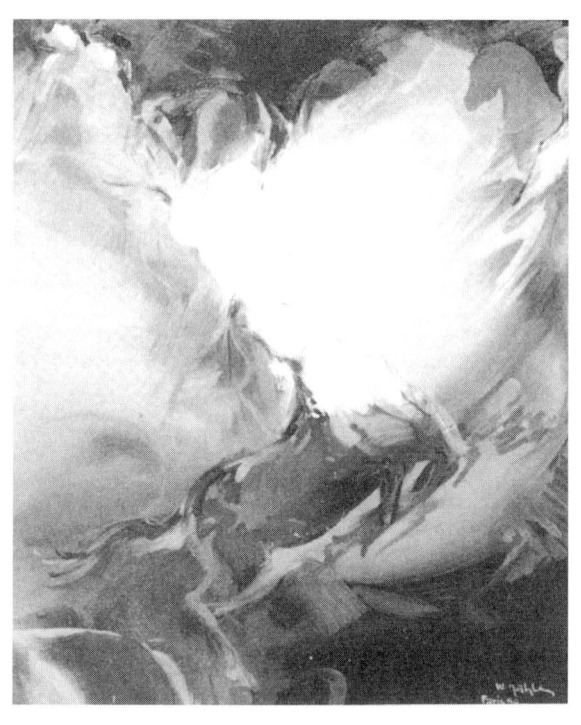

❖ 65 ❖

تلألأَتْ تحت جفنِك، لم تنفرْ.
هَبَطَتْ في قلبي الى الأبد.

The fleeting tear in your eye
wasn't startled.
It landed in my heart to stay forever.

Sous ta paupière, scintilla une larme.
Elle ne déferla pas.
Mon cœur en fut imbibé pour toujours.

Unter deinem Lid glänzte eine Träne.
Sie trat nicht hervor,
sondern landete für immer
in meinem Herzen.

❖ 66 ❖

تَهُبِّين في قلبي كشرارةٍ تتقمَّص .

You keep breathing into my heart.
That's why the sparks keep reigniting.

Etincelle, en perpétuelle incarnation,
tu surgis dans mon cœur.

Du hauchst in mein Herz.
Der Funke entfacht.

❖ 67 ❖

وَعَدْتِ أَنَّكِ آتِيَة. ثُمَّ لم.
كَأَنَّكِ جِئْتِ. نِيَّتُكِ مَجِيءٌ.

You promised you'd be here but no.
You meant to come.
It's as if you did.

Tu as promis de venir.
Mais ... Comme si tu étais venue.
C'était dans ton intention.

Du versprachst, hier zu sein,
du kamst nicht.
Dein Vorsatz war ein Kommen.

❖ 68 ❖

*All of my tomorrows – their memory
nothing but you.*

*A chacun de mes lendemains,
Tu en es la mémoire.*

*Von all meinen künftigen Tagen ist
es die Erinnerung an dich, die zählt.*

❖ 69 ❖

قبلَكِ، كَان الوصولُ أُفقَ غياب.

معَكِ، يَتَرَنْبَقُ انتظاراً للفجرِ التالي.

Before you
wherever I arrived was a vista of loss.
With you
just waiting blooms into
a white-tuliped dawn.

Avant toi, L'union comptait:
Horizon au crépuscule.
Avec toi, elle fleurit tel un lys
attente de l'aube suivante.

Vor dir: am Horizont erschien
stets eine Abwesenheit.
Mit dir: liliengleich blüht
das Erwarten des Morgens.

70

يقولون جمالَكِ، وأعرفُـه.
وأُحِبُّ أن أَكتشِفَـهُ،
عبر عيونهـم،
كلَّ مرّة.

They talk about your beauty,
and I know it myself.
But I love to rediscover it
using their eyes.

Je connais ta beauté
Ils la racontent.
J'aime la découvrir,
Au travers leurs yeux, à chaque fois.

Sie sprechen über deine Schönheit,
die ich kenne.
Doch liebe ich es, sie durch ihre
Augen stets neu zu entdecken.

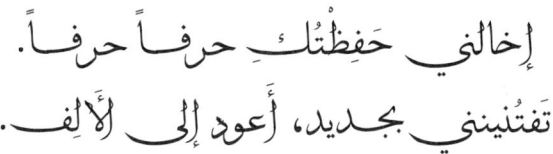

71

I thought I had studied you
letter by letter ...
then you would infatuate me again
and I was back at alif.

Il me semble t'avoir retenue lettre
après lettre.
Je retourne à la lettre A.
Et tu me séduis à nouveau.

Ich glaubte, dich entziffert zu haben,
Buchstaben für Buchstaben.
Dann betörst du mich aufs neue,
und ich kehre zurück zum
Buchstaben A.

❖ 72 ❖

كلَّ مرّةٍ أوّلُ مرّة.
كلَّ يومٍ أوّلُ يومٍ.
ما أُكثَرَكِ !

Every time the first time.
Every day the first day.
How many "yous" there are!

Chaque fois est une première.
Chaque jour est le premier.
Combien tu es plusieurs!

Jedes Mal ist das erste Mal.
Jeder Tag der erste Tag.
Wie vielfältig bist du!

❖ 73 ❖

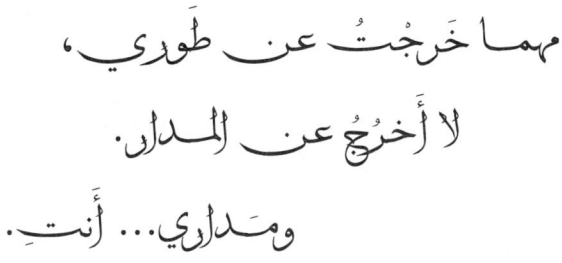

مهما خَرَجْتُ عن طَوري،
لا أَخرُجُ عن المَدار.
ومَداري... أَنتِ.

I may step out of my usual course,
but never from my orbit.
You are that orbit.

Quelque soit ma colère,
je ne quitte guère la trajectoire.
Tu es ... mon orbite.

So sehr ich aus mir herausgehe,
nie verlasse ich meine Umlaufbahn.
Meine Umlaufbahn bist du.

❖ 74 ❖

كُلَّمَا دلّلْتُكِ أَقـلّ،
ضاق صـدري.
عَطَائيلكِ الحُبّ،
تَنَفُّسي الأقصى.

When attention to you lapses
my heart contracts in my breast.
The more I love you the deeper I breathe.

Si peu te câliner m'étouffe
Offrande d'amour, mon extrême respiration.

Wenn meine Aufmerksamkeit nachlässt,
verspannt sich mein Herz,
angesichts deiner Liebe entspannt es sich.

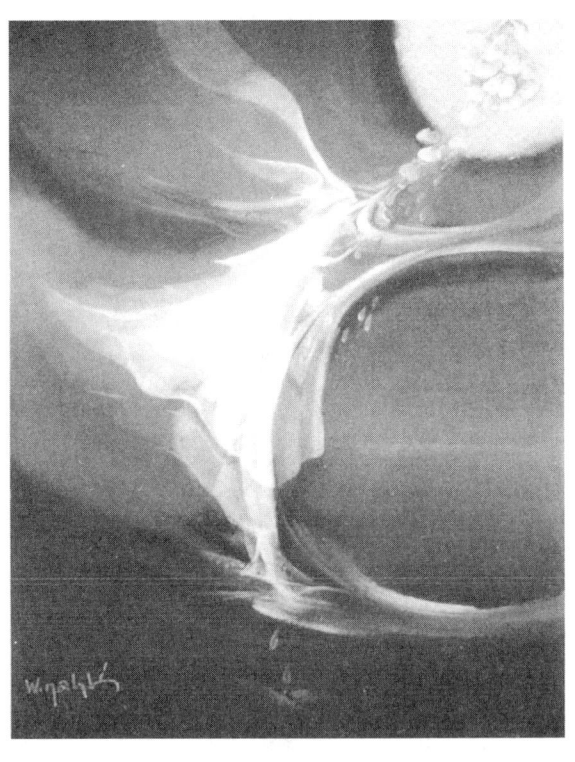

❖ 75 ❖

إِذَا انتظَارُيكِ الطَّريقُ،
فَوَعدُكِ الوُصولُ لأَجمَلُ.

If waiting is an endless path,
the promise of your arrival becomes
still more beautiful.

T'attendre, certes, est le chemin,
Ta promesse est la plus belle rencontre.

Wenn das Warten auf dich der Weg ist,
so ist das Versprechen deiner Ankunft
die schönste Begegnung.

❖ 76 ❖

بعــد، بعــد...

وأعرف أنني لن أرتوي.

Again, and yet again,
although I know too well,
I'll never have enough.

Encore, encore.
Je sais combien je reste inassouvi.

Wieder und immer wieder ...
Ich weiss genau, ich werde
nie gesättigt sein.

❖ 77 ❖

شوقُكِ أَشـدُّ بُرَكاناً... أَمِ انتظاري؟

Which eruption is the more powerful?
Your yearning or my waiting?

Plus fort qu'un volcan:
Ton désir envers moi
Ou bien que je t'attende?

Ist es deine Sehnsucht,
die stärker ist als ein Vulkan
oder meine Erwartung?

❖ 78 ❖

جمالُكِ الزيتون المبارك...
أَشُمَّهُ، أَتبارُكَ بزيته المقدَّس.

Your beauty is the holy olive grove.
I breathe it in to anoint myself.

Olivier béni, ta beauté
Je la sens, je suis béni de l'huile sacrée.

Deine Schönheit ist
ein geweihter Ölbaum.
Ich atme tief ein und bin desalbt
mit heiligem Öl.

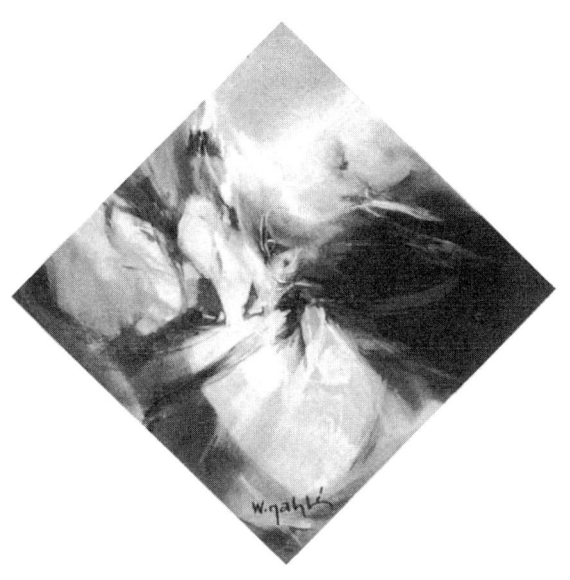

 79 ❖

أيَّتُهـا الكَّثيرةُ الصمتِ...
مـا أُكثَر أَبجديَّاتِك!

You of the many silences.
How numerous are your alphabets.

Ô toi auguste silencieuse
Innombrables sont tes alphabets.

Du Schweigsame ...
Wie zahlreich sind deine Alphabete!

❖ 80 ❖

كلُّ شهقـةٍ سنونوّةٌ يَتَموسَم بهـا ربيـع.

Every sigh a swallow darting through,
seasoning the spring.

Chaque soupir est une hirondelle ...
Un printemps s'y annonce aux saisons

Jeder Seufzer eine Schwalbe,
die den Frühling ankündigt.

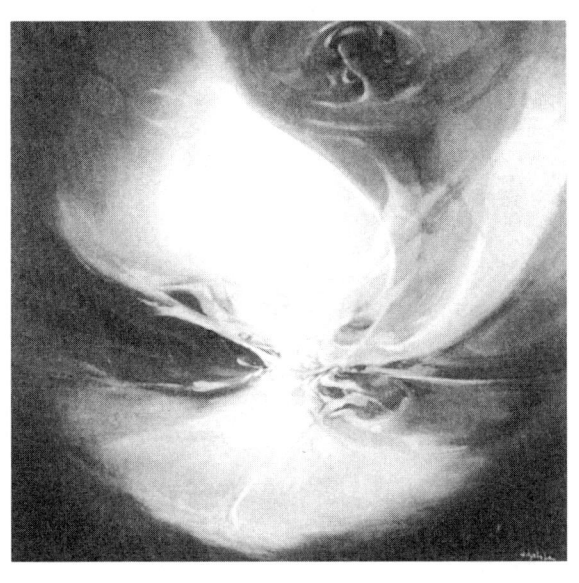

هــذا البياض... هــذا البياض...
أبجــديةُ الصبح وفهرسُ القبلة !

This dazzling whiteness ...
is the alphabet of morning,
the afterword of a kiss.

Liliale ... Liliale cette blancheur
Alphabet du matin
Lexique du baiser

Diese weiße Stelle ...
Alphabet des Morgens
Nachwort des Kusses.

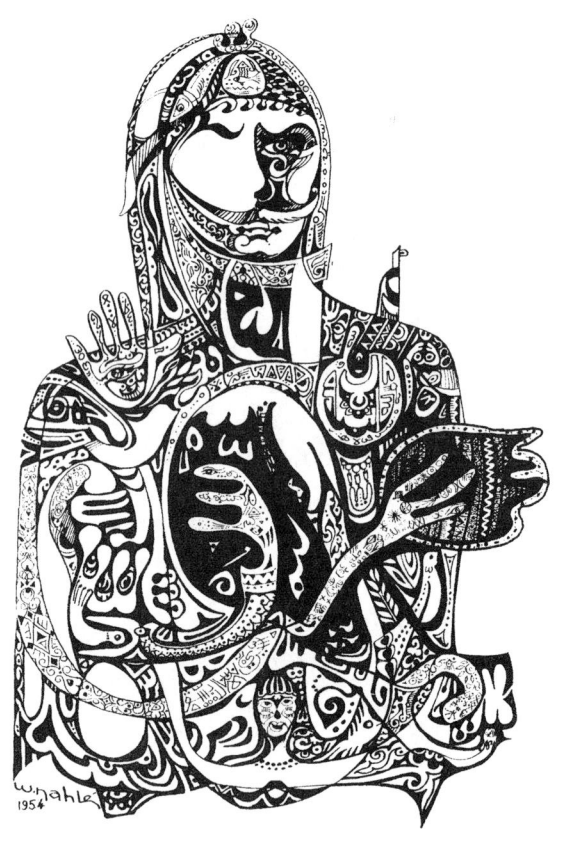

❖ 82 ❖

هــذا الكوثر، نبع الحيــاة
الأطهر الأعذب الأنقى ...
شرايني له، وفمي .

This living water font of life,
purest, sweetest, clearest.
I give my mouth to it.
Let it flow in my veins.

Ce nectar, source de vie la plus pure
La plus délicieuse et la plus claire
Je lui dédie
Mes veines avec ma bouche aussi.

Dieser Paradiesfluß, reinste,
köstlichste, klarste Lebensquelle ...
ich biete ihm meine Venen
und meinen Mund.

❖ 83 ❖

لأنني دائماً في اشتياقٍ لاهبٍ،
يُخجلني حضوري بركانٍ أقلّ.

My yearning is always on fire.
When we finally meet
if the flame is low, I get embarrassed.

Comme je suis tout le temps
Désirant, enflammé
J'ai la honte, quand le volcan
De ma présence, devant toi, se tiédit.

Da meine Sehnsucht immer entflammt ist,
beschämt es mich, wenn der Vulkan
in deiner Gegenwart erkaltet.

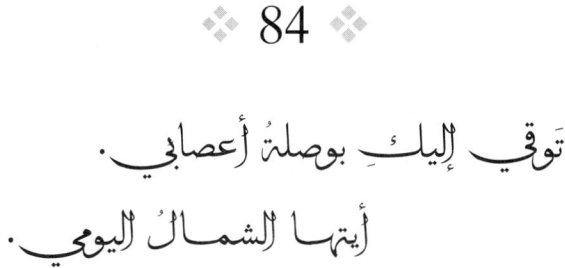

❖ 84 ❖

تَوقِي إِلَيكِ بوصلةُ أَعصابي .

أَيتها الشمالُ اليومي .

My longing for you
is my internal compass.
It always points north.

Te désirer est la boussole de mes nerfs,
Ô Toi ; mon nord quotidien.

Meine Sehnsucht nach dir
ist mein innerer Kompass.
Du bist mein täglicher Norden.

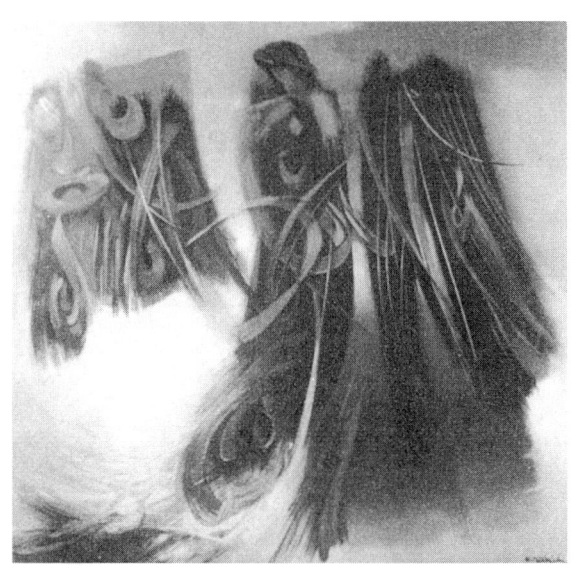

❖ 85 ❖

أَجْمَلُ مَا في حُبِّنَا... لِمَاذَاهُ.

The most beautiful aspect of our love ...
its why.

Le plus beau de notre amour:
Le pourquoi.

Das Schönste unserer Liebe ...
das Warum

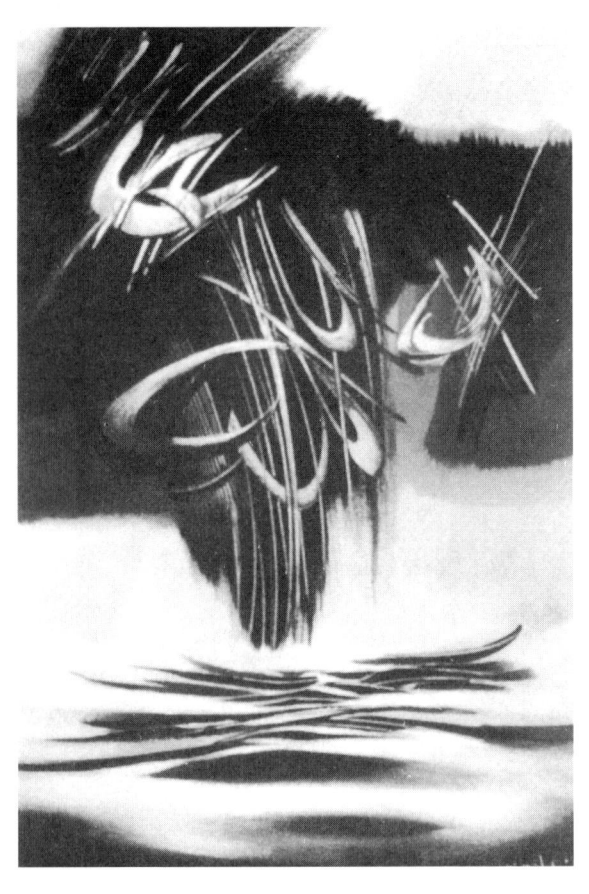

❖ 86 ❖

شوقٌ في غيابكِ...

انشـــدادٌ في حضوركِ...

أيـــن أنــا؟؟؟

Longing when you're away.
Gravitation towards you when you're here.
Where do I fit in?

Désir en ton absence …
Attirance en ta présence …
Où suis-je???

Sehnsucht in deiner Abwesenheit ...
Anziehung in deiner Gegenwart ...
Wo bin ich???

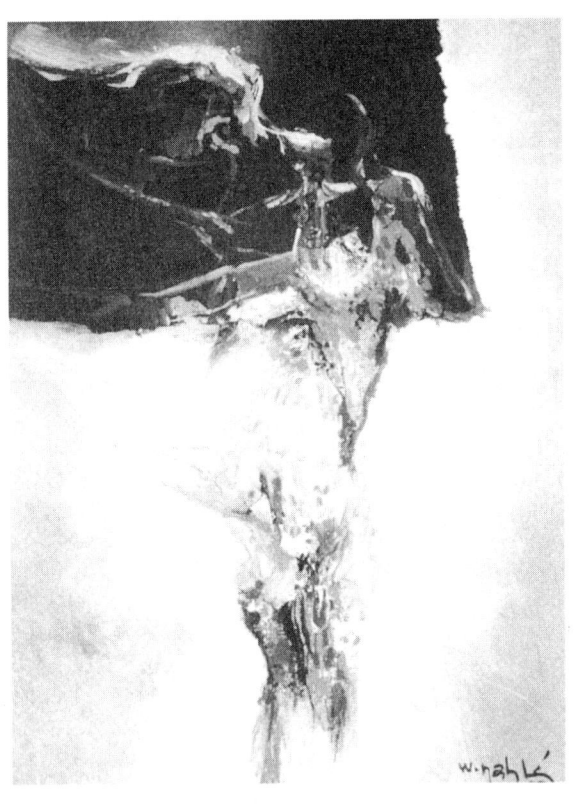

❖ 87 ❖

أُغْنُجِي ... أُغْنُجِي ... وَلْيَطُلْ عُمْرِي!

Keep teasing me. I'll live longer.

Sois caline, sois caline,
Mon âge se prolongera ...

Schmeichle mir,
Ich werde länger leben.

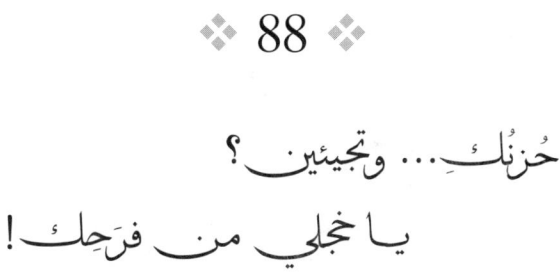

In spite of your grief, you come by.
How could I manage
when you were happy?

Triste et tu viens?
Que je me méprise face à ta joie!

Trotz deiner Traurigkeit kommst du?
Deine Freude machte mich verlegen.

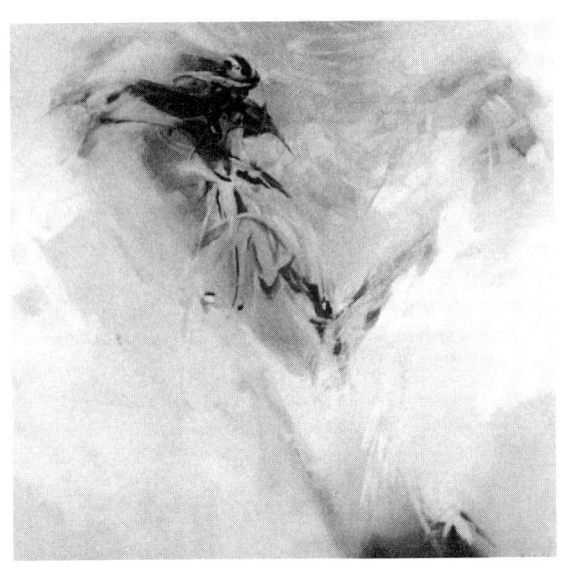

❖ 89 ❖

لو دُوارُكِ إعصاري...
لأَذوقَ دوّامةَ تقصيري في حبّك !

If a change in you caused a storm in me,
I would know why the whirlpool of my love
was not strong enough.

Si ton vertige m'était tourbillon ...
Je goûterais,
Labyrinthe d'être en court de ton amour.

Dein Zögern bewirkt einen Sturm in mir.
Das Nachlassen deiner Liebe,
welch einen Wirbel!

❖ 90 ❖

وأَعظمُ تضحياتِكِ، ...
أن تُضحي سعادتي.

The greatest offering of your love:
your sacrifice for my happiness.

Que tu façonnes mon bonheur
Est le plus grand de tes sacrifices.

Das grösste Opfer deiner Liebe,
mein Glück zu bewirken.

❖ 91 ❖

أيتها الآتية إلى مستقبلي،
اختصري ماضيَّ الحاضِر.

Since you lead me into my future,
make my ever present past shorter.

Ô Toi, allant vers mon futur
Epargne-moi mon passé omniprésent.

Die du in meine Zukunft kommst,
kürze meine gegenwärtige
Vergangenheit ab!

❖ 92 ❖

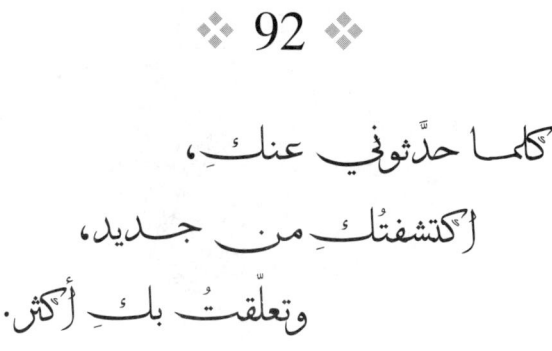

كلّما حدّثوني عنكِ،
اكتشفتُكِ من جديد،
وتعلّقتُ بكِ أكثر.

They talk to me about you.
I just discover more
and cling to you more closely still.

Dès qu'on me parle de toi,
Je renouvelle ma découverte,
Je m'attache à toi de plus en plus.

Sie sprechen über dich,
ich entdecke mehr von dir
und bin dir mehr und mehr zugetan.

❖ 93 ❖

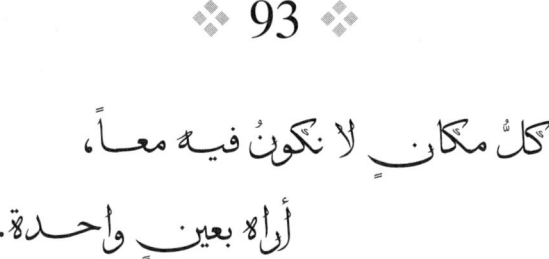

كلُّ مكانٍ لا نكونُ فيه معاً،
أراه بعينٍ واحـدة.

Every place I go without you
looking with one eye is enough.

D'un oeil orphelin
Je vois l'espace qui ne nous réunit pas.

Für jeden Platz,
den ich ohne dich aufsuche,
brauche ich nur ein Auge.

❖ 94 ❖

مــا أُطيبَـه بْكراً قبـل الرحيـق،
ولو عـن شحـوبِ تَعَـب.

How delicious your wine
before it's fully aged,
even if it's a little pale,
not yet full-bodied.

Ton visage premier
Synonyme d'une pâleur fatiguée,
Qu'il est délicieux
Avant la sève.

Wie köstlich ist der junge Wein
trotz seiner noch blassen Farbe.

❖ 95 ❖

... وتلتقي شفـاهُنا على قبلةٍ

تمتدُّ ألفَ عـامٍ!

And so our lips meet in a kiss.
It lingers for a thousand years.

Le baiser qui souda nos lèvres
S'étalera une éternité.

Unsere Lippen begegneten
sich in einem Kuss,
der tausend Jahre währt.

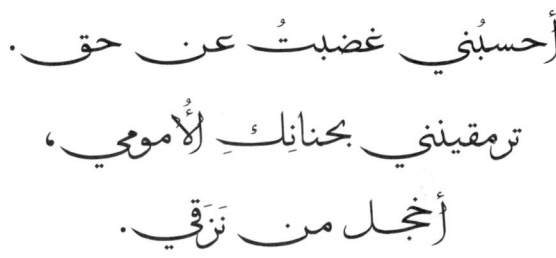

96

أَحسبُني غَضبتُ عن حقٍّ .

ترمقيني بِحنانِكِ الأُمومي ،

أَخجَلُ من نَزَقي .

I consider myself right to be angry with you.
After all, your glance towards me,
full of maternal tenderness,
makes me more aware of my own
thoughtlessness.

Il me semble que ma colère soit juste
Un regard de toi bienveillant d'une mère
me rend à moi-même.
Et je me méprise dans ma fougue.

Ich hielt es für gerecht, dir zu zürnen;
doch ein Blick voll mütterlicher
Zärtlichkeit von dir,
und ich bedauere meine Voreiligkeit.

97

هــذه الضمَّـة القصيرة...
أطول لذّةٍ لنشوة الروح!

It's a short embrace,
but for the soul's ecstasy it is
the longest lasting of pleasures.

Etreinte furtive,
Le plus long plaisir
de l'exaltation de l'âme!

Kurzes Umarmen,
doch das längste Vergnügen
für die Ekstase der Seele.

❖ 98 ❖

طيفلكِ تحـت المطرِ،
ضوءٌ هامسٌ لصحو الربيع !

Your shadow under the rain –
light whispering to the clarity of spring.

Ta silhouette sous la pluie,
Eclair murmurant le réveil du printemps!

Deine Gestalt im Regen,
Flüsterndes Licht zum Wecken des Frühlings.

هذا النعاس على وجهكِ الملائكي،
وعـدُ الضوء قبـل نقطةِ الفجر.

This lingering tiredness
of your ethereal face:
a promise of light before the blink of dawn.

Sommeil sur ton visage angélique
Promesse de la lumière,
Avant le point de l'aube.

Schläfrigkeit auf deinem Engelsgesicht,
Lichtverheissung vor Anbruch
der Morgendämmerung.

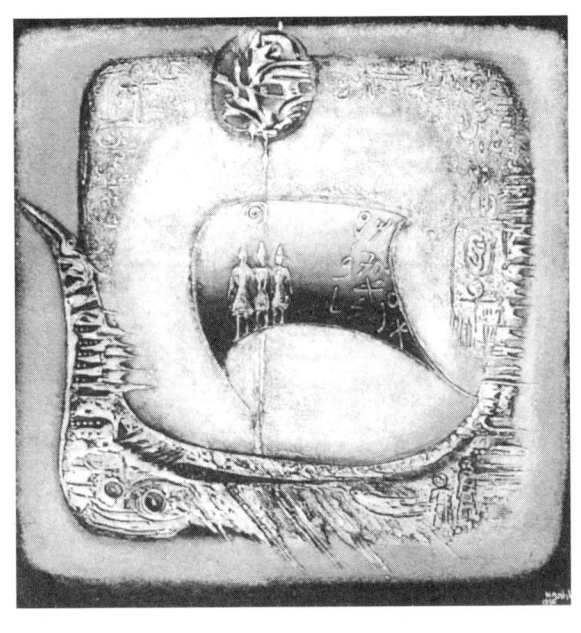

❖ 100 ❖

يا سِرَّكِ المُغْلَق... متى يَفتَحُ لي؟

This undisclosed mystery of yours –
when does it open for me?

Ô ton secret-coffré ...
Quand m'ouvrira-t-il?

Dein verschlossenes Geheimnis ...
Wann wird es sich mir öffnen?